DO YOUR

DAMN JOB!

Do Your Damn Job

Jeff Dawson

DO YOUR DAMN JOB!

JEFF DAWSON

Mr. Dawson is the author of over eighteen works. His memoir, dedicated to his high school sweetheart, "Love's True Second Chance" was awarded the seal of approval from the IndiePendent Association for exemplary story writing. A full list can be found at the end of this work.

He currently live in the Dallas/Fort Worth Area.

Copyright © 2019 by: LDDJ Enterprises Publishing

ISBN: 978-1-7321547-3-5

All rights reserved, including the right to reproduce this book or portions thereof in any form or by any means, electronic or mechanical, including photocopying, recording, or by any information storage and retrieval system without permission in writing from the author. All inquiries should be addressed to LDDJ Enterprises Publishing, 1055 Regal Row #314, Dallas, TX. 75247.

Jeff Dawson

All the events describe did happen. In some cases, names of companies or individuals have been changed for privacy issues.

Table of Contents

Intro	7
1) Partnering	10
2) Meetings	20
3) Accountability	38
4) Bad Advice, Incompetents and Brown Nosers	48
5) Confrontation and Respect	59
6) Team	80
7) Church Social	85
8) Bad Bosses	89
9) Let's Have a Beer	94
10) Live to Work, Work to live?	99
11) Praise	103
12) Aftermath	105

Jeff Dawson

INTRO

It is better to offer no excuse than a bad one.

George Washington

What pray tell, is this book about?

Simple, Read the title.

Any questions? No? Well, then you've already set yourself up for failure.

"Who me? I never make a mistake!"

Try again. If you aren't making a mistake then you aren't trying. You're too scared to take a risk and stick with it.

Do I have your attention yet?

This book is a no-nonsense look at managing employees. I won't pull punches, sugar coat it or do one of the biggest mistakes I see in self-help books, I won't talk at you. I will talk to you in plain, everyday language.

I have spent over thirty-five years in the construction industry; laborer, operator, foreman, superintendent, project manager and business owner. In that time, I have seen some of the most dysfunctional management techniques known to man to run projects

I'm not going go into a lot of theory and hip techniques that business schools are pushing because, honestly, I don't give a damn. You make the work environment simple, comfortable and efficient, or, you can choose the opposite and fill the office with political bullshit and a lot of buzz words which will lead to low morale, poor productivity and general unrest. Doesn't sound very appetizing to me.

If you feel you just got ripped, that is not my intention. Rather, I'm setting the table for how we as mangers need to address our everyday assignments, delegating authority and communicating with employees and bosses.

Jeff Dawson

We are going to cover the following areas: getting organized, being prepared for meetings, conducting meetings, accountability, interacting with employees, dealing with conflict, handling bad bosses and employees, praising good performance and last but not least, how to keep our sanity in an insane world.

Are you ready? I am. Let's go!

PARTNERING

Who remembers when this was all the rage in the business world? I do and all I can say is, it was the biggest waste of time and money the City of Dallas put on the taxpayers in an indirect way. It was a bid item for each project. Thus, the taxpayers had no idea what they were paying for. Thinking all of their bond money was going to building improvements for the residents, a portion of it was going to feed employees who would never have a thing to do with the project and let us not leave out the consultants who were charging for their expertise. If memory serves me right, the initial fee was $1500.00! That might not seem like a lot of money. It's not, as long as you get what was promised by the description of "Partnering" in the specification book.

This is what it looks like on the surface. The consultant will create a separate company, with an approved logo by all parties, contractor, city and consultant. The logo will be proudly displayed on the project sign so the public knows who's running the show. This shell company, in theory, will be the clearing house for all problems arising during the construction of the project. Basically, they will be a mediator when the contractor and city can't resolve outstanding issues. You got it, conflict resolution!

Sounds like a good idea doesn't it? Let's see how well it worked.

The meeting was held at Pappadeaux's Seafood in the Cedar Springs area of Dallas, TX. Who do you think picked it out? Not me. The consultant. Okay, I can deal with this. Since I'm paying for it let's see, I've got $5,000.00 in the bid item. $1,500 for the consultant. Not bad. Now let's do a headcount. Each plate should run say, $55.00.

Attendees: Contractor 2, Consultant 1, City of Dallas- Project manager 1, Construction Inspector 1, Inspector 1,

Consultant engineer 1 maybe 2. They might bring a junior engineer with them for the experience. No problem. OMBO might send a person. Oh, that's Office of Minority Business Opportunity and last but not least the city surveyor. Let's see, that is a total of 10. So, $1500.00 plus $550 totals $2,050.00 leaving $2,950.00 profit. Sounds like a solid number doesn't it? Try again. There were at least twenty-five people at the meeting! Who they were and why they were attending was my initial reaction? Instead of addressing this immediately, I decided to ride it out and then make an appropriate comment when the time was right.

The consultant opened the meeting, introducing herself and pouring on more accolades than I cared to hear about. Yep, she's already losing me. Then came the introduction for all of the attendees: name, company, function, likes, dislikes etc. This is when I found out who many of those who weren't invited were from. Yep. Made a note of those individuals.

Let me take a break for a minute before I delve into what occurred during this fine exchange of intellectual exchanges.

Why did the City of Dallas have to hire a partnering firm to conduct a preconstruction meeting? That was the question of the day.

Prior to this, we would sit down with the Engineer of record, who was a City of Dallas employee, all of the utility companies which had easement and equipment that could interfere with the construction activities, the area inspector and the inspector who would be responsible for the project and of course, the contractor. That's it. What's that, ten people? Close enough.

These meetings were productive and informative. All aspects of the project were addressed. Any potential conflicts were examined immediately. The goal was to get the job built on time and minimize the inconvenience to local businesses and commuters. The system worked!

Let me repeat that, THE SYSTEM WORKED! And then something horrible and outrageous happened. The city decided to outsource their engineering department to consultants. They said it would streamline jobs and be more cost efficient for the owner. It might have been cost efficient for the owner, but I'm here to tell you it DID NOT streamline the jobs at all.

Back to the meeting.

After an hour or so of the consultant explaining how this grand scheme was going to work, she did some half ass slide show. That's how interested I was.

Then came the dreaded personality quiz. How many books have you read of late on management techniques that allude to the test or talking openly about your likes and dislikes? You know what I'm talking about. Are you a Type A, B, C, D, or even Z personality? Your guess is as good as mine what the Z could stand for. Better ask someone with a PHD who's smarter than me on this one. Alright, back on point.

Believe it or not, I have a Type A personality. What a shocker! But that wasn't the fun part. It was when the consultant started describing each personality based on her in-depth experience in construction, which was zero and her heady research, which was lacking. When she said that type A personalities didn't like to read, I'd had enough of this crap. My assistant project manager noticed I was getting hot under the collar.

"Jeff, don't do it. Don't do it."

"Why?"

"We have to work with these people."

"I don't care. She's isn't going to stand up there and tell me what I do and don't like."

"Okay."

Should I have listened to my colleague's sage advice? Perhaps. But that isn't in my make up when someone makes an erroneous statement with nothing to back it up. So, I told her real quick that her research was crap and I would not listen to any more of this foolishness. I am an avid reader and amateur historian. The look on her face was priceless. Her response, "Maybe I need to do some more research." Ya think?

For most of the meeting I'd been a good boy and kept my mouth shut. I gave her a chance to pitch this new idea and see if it had any merit. But after three hours of nonsense, I'd had enough.

As she wound down, patting herself on the back for such a stellar presentation, she gave me the door I'd been waiting all afternoon to crash through.

"Are there any questions?' She said this while starting to pack up her items.

Jeff Dawson

I'm sure many of you, when you hear that question, know that the meeting is winding down and you can't wait to leave. Of course not. You got a free lunch and weren't responsible for what just transpired. I believe some of the attendees were starting to get up when I said.

"Yes. I have a couple of questions. We have sat here for over three hours and have yet to accomplish anything of value." Can anyone relate to what I just blurted out? "One, I would like to know why all of these people are here? I've never seen half of them and seeing how I've done projects with the City for the last fifteen years; I know all the players. So, who are they and why were they here?" The question slapped everyone in the room. Remember, I'm paying for this.

"No answers. I'm shocked. Now let's get down to what this waste of time was supposed to address. One, am I going to be paid on time and two, will my questions concerning the project be addressed in a timely fashion? That's it. That's all I want to know."

The consultant turned to the multitude of City representatives and divested to them. Guess what their answer was? Go ahead. Take a guess. The response. "We can't guarantee they will be paid on time or that rfi's (request for information) will be answered in a timely fashion."

"Really? Then why in the hell did we spend almost four hours, discussing and resolving nothing! This has been the biggest waste of time I've ever been a part of and a huge waste of taxpayers' money."

The consultant suggested we have another meeting to resolve the issues. You already know what my answer was don't you?

Here's the point I'm driving home, the city was conned into buying into a "new concept" that was untried and unproven and ultimately failed. They won't admit that, but it's a fact.

How does this relate to your situation? Simple. Stick with what works. The simpler the better. Only have those who belong in a meeting at the meeting. They are not to be a free-for-all and when your come to the meeting, be prepared to address all of the important issues. Will they all be resolved in the first sit down? No. For those issues that cannot be resolved, at least the ground work has been laid out for it to be tackled at a future meeting.

MEETINGS

Did you think a management book wouldn't have a chapter about meetings? Were you hoping I wouldn't bring up this word of taboo? Or maybe you were hoping of all hope that based on my no BS attitude I would be the last person to discuss meetings especially after that inspiring one with the City of Dallas. Well, you would be wrong because I'm going to give a whole new perspective on how to conduct one and be prepared when you walk in so it won't be a waste of your time or mine. Believe me, I hate meetings just as much as the next person because ninety percent of the them accomplish nothing other than people taking notes and planning on the next meeting. This won't happen with my style-guaranteed!

Instead of giving one example, it's necessary to give multiple ones. Each one has a unique issue, but the resolutions were the same because I walked in prepared for bear.

On the US 75 job, we had a unique problem. The amount of underground utilities conflicting with the installation of the new conduit was thicker than the coffee Eva Gabor fixed Ollie in the television show, "Green Acres." If you aren't familiar with the show, then try threading a camel through the eye of a needle. On top of the utilities, the City of Richardson has just spent over a million dollars on a landscape beautification project that, you guessed it, was smack dab in the middle of the new conduit runs. That problem was resolved with not a lot of effort. The state agreed to let us bore the majority of these areas and pay us the extra money. The utility conflict problem wasn't so easy. Let me point out before I go on. Before the project started, John and I spent two weeks talking to the cities: Allen, Plano and Richardson and the utility companies on marking their lines. We spent a week marking out the proposed lines, so when the utility companies marked theirs, we could see all the conflicts.

John and I spent one Sunday filming the entire fifteen miles. I took the tape back and converted it to a CD. I then put together a seven-page report detailing all the conflicts. Copies were given to the state, the engineers, the cities and my boss. Guess what action was taken? None!

A year later the problem still remained because no one wanted to address the problem when it was identified. Why they didn't is the real question here. Any one relate to this situation? Now some might get discouraged that their hard work was being over looked. You would be wrong. We did our due diligence and that is something to be proud of because it isn't going to go away or fix itself. Victory will be ours before it's all said and done. Wait and see.

The only logical solution was to hang the conduit on the bridges. This idea was shot down faster than Doc Holiday taking out Johnny Ringo. It would be aesthetically unpleasing to the motorists. That was a lame excuse for me, but okay, now what? The state wanted ideas.

There's another issue I need to add to the equation. These conduits would have fiber lines being pulled through them and when you pull fiber you cannot have a 360 degree turn anywhere on the line. If it happens, the fiber will break during the pulling operation and that's a whole different problem we don't want to have happen.

The State suggested we bore under Beltline and Arapaho. Good idea with one problem, how many trees can we remove to perform the bores? Answer-none.

I was out of ideas. John and Jose had nothing.

The owner of the company decided to get involved. Fair enough, it's his firm. Let's see if he has a feasible solution.

All of the parties drove the job and made notes. The solutions everyone came up with were good ones. Or so they thought. For once I kept my mouth shut and listened to everyone's suggestions. They would move the conduit and some bores to avoid the conflicts. Instead of the pipe being on the outside of the service road lanes, the lines would be placed in the available medians, bypassing all those pesky lines.

I will give credit where credit is due. They did manage to build ninety-five percent of project. It was the last five percent they weren't looking at.

After they finished shaking hands and back-slapping each other on a job well done, the owner looked at me.

"Jeff, you haven't said anything. Is there a problem?"

"As a matter of fact, Mr. Kevin I want to congratulate all of you for almost building the entire job. I think it's wonderful what has been accomplished today. There's one small issue I need to point out before you start pouring the champagne."

You could see their jaws drop and that look of dejection sweeping across their faces.

"Where we're standing, we have a bore to install."

"And your point?"

"Well, I'm standing on top of a phone vault that is eight feet deep. In order for us to go under the vault the bore would have to be about twelve feet deep."

"And?" He just kept fueling the fire.

"In order to not kink the fiber on the pull, the bore will come up about one hundred feet to the west." I looked at Sam the State's project manager. "Sam, these flags here. Are they the property line?"

"Yes."

"So, you don't own the land where the bore will come out of the ground?"

"No."

"Does the State plan on buying the property anytime soon?"

"No."

"Then gentlemen, I don't think what you proposed will work."

And that was it. The project was shut down for six months until the State could figure out what to do and guess what we did? If you guessed we hung that unsightly conduit on the bridges you would be correct.

The sad part is all of this could have been resolved before the project started when I handed out the CD and notes, denoting all of the problems we would encounter.

I didn't dwell on the multiple meetings that were held to resolve the issue because as you can see, they were fruitless until they, the State was faced with a problem that wouldn't go away.

In a sense it was a victory for me and my staff because we were prepared and could support our position. If only those who made the decisions would have taken appropriate action before it became a serious problem, a whole lot of time and money would not have been wasted.

It would have been easy to give up and succumb to the pressure I was receiving; it would have been the easy thing to do but it would have been the wrong one.

The second meeting was classic. On the 635 project, the structure company called and informed me there was a problem with the size of the structures. The ones designed weren't going to work with the clearances required on the highway. I told him, I'd look into it. This was John's specialty so I did the logical thing and turned it over to him. It took him about a day to examine the problem. He concurred. The structure wouldn't work.

Before moving forward a little background is necessary. The structures I'm referring to are the ones on the highway with the big green signs on them. They consist of a drilled pier, pier steel, anchor bolts, legs and the truss.

The size of the drilled pier is based on height, length, wind resistance and size of sign. This determines the size of a pier to be drilled and the other items mentioned. Drilling the pier is the easy part. Getting the steel, anchor bolts, legs and trusses all have to be fabricated and that can take anywhere from six to ten weeks depending on the supplier's schedule.

When John verified the findings, I informed the contractor we had a problem. He too checked the structure and agreed, there was a problem. Okay, we have all the powers to be working in the same direction. The contractor suggested we check all of the structures before moving forward. He was going to notify the State of the problem.

I developed a neat little formula that would do all the calculations for the structures. Out of forty-five structures, thirty weren't going to work. The information was forwarded to the contractor who notified the State we needed a meeting with them and the engineering firm.

Based on our findings, thirty were going to have to be redesigned. The original ones were too small. This is going to result in a substantial change order for the extra sizing. The cost for doing a 54", 48" drill shaft versus a 36" drill shaft is considerable.

This was the first time in a long time the subcontractor, contractor, supplier and State were convinced there was a problem and the engineer of record needed to correct it.

At the meeting, the head engineer for the firm was in attendance. If you've never worked with an engineer before, you're in for a treat. We presented our facts and informed him of how many of the structures required a redesign. He scoffed at our findings and said, "If my junior engineer was here, he would stand behind his designs."

I retorted. "And our supplier, who's been building these for the last fifty years stands behind our findings that thirty of your structures are wrong."

Let me tell you what. That arrogant engineer had nothing. He did say that there might be a problem with five, but not thirty. Instead of admitting there was a problem he dismissed us and walked out. In the end, we received new prints for thirty structures.

This was another successful meeting, because it took less than an hour and action was being taken. There were no more meetings on this topic. The reason it was successful is we were prepared and weren't backing down.

I cannot stress enough how important it is to be thoroughly prepared and ready to defend your position no matter who you're meeting with. Even if those you are talking to don't share your same viewpoint, if your facts are solid and you don't question them, nine times out of ten you are going to come out on the winning side for all parties involved.

Jeff Dawson

The last meeting I want to cover is one that did not turn out well. It was a duct bank project at a university campus in Richardson. When the project was awarded to our firm, I posed a simple question to the GC, who is going to locate utilities in the work areas? Some of the lines were going to be in the ROW and easements that DIGG Tess will mark. But who was going to mark the utilities on the campus? City or the University? They said they would look into it. The question was posed at least two more times before the dirt crew moved in. Since I wasn't involved with the dirt portion of the project, it wasn't my problem. My boss was handling it.

The first day they started moving dirt, they hit a fiber line and just missed the power line. The shit hit the fan. The GC wanted my boss at their office first thing in the morning. No excuses. He asked me to attend the meeting. I didn't think I would be able to add much, but agreed to his request.

I need to point out that the issue of locates was never addressed by the GC after discussing it at two previous meetings. When we started the work, the lines were not properly marked.

We show up and the GC and my boss spent over an hour discussing how to resolve the issue by working up more reports and having more meetings to discuss the previous meetings findings and what topics to cover at the next meeting all the while not addressing the issue at hand.

As it appeared the brainstorming, paper pushing extravaganza was about to end my boss looked at me. "Jeff. You haven't said anything. What do you think about our solutions?"

This door should have never been opened. For once, I probably should have kept my mouth shut and agreed with them, but that's not my nature. I looked down at my watch and began. "Gentlemen, we've been here an hour and ten minutes and yet no one has addressed the problem.

You've discussed filling out more reports and having more meetings on the reports but you have yet to identity who is going to locate the lines and correct me if I'm wrong, that's why we're here today. Correct? Until all the lines are properly marked by the City the University or the Utility provider, I'm recommending to my boss not to move another yard of dirt. I'm just glad we didn't hit a power line or the gas line that is clearly visible and kill someone. And gentlemen, I covered the important issue in less than five minutes. Now, what are you going to do?"

Was my analysis of the problem resolution correct? Yes. Was the delivery well received? Absolutely not. Some GC's are more arrogant than engineers. Tell them they're wrong and they will make your life miserable because by God, they don't make mistakes and they'll be damned if some piss ant subcontractor is going to call them out.

Would I do it again? Yes. But what I wouldn't do is sign the sub-contract. I had a bad feeling before our firm signed the contract and that feeling proved out in the end.

If I would have trusted my gut, I would have done a better job of warning my boss about what I thought we were walking into. That was my mistake and I take full responsibility for it.

As you can see, meetings aren't a bad thing if you are properly prepared and not afraid of ruffling feathers. It might not make you the most popular person in the room, but you will be the most respected and that is worth its weight in gold.

The last example wasn't exactly a meeting but I'm going to really drive home the point of being prepared.

The company I worked was labor driven. That's all they cared about. How much are you spending in labor each week. They didn't care about equipment, depreciation, materials, supplies, fuel, maintenance or repair costs; only labor.

I'd been with company about a year and-a-half and we were jamming. Had at least fifteen crews working on three different projects. Each one was on time and under budget.

Each week I entered the payroll and put together a draft estimate so I knew what direction we were headed. Overall, the labor for the projects came in around twelve percent of the contract total. My numbers showed labor was coming in around eight percent. That's pretty damn good.

My boss called me up.

"Jeff, this is Jim. I need to ask you a few questions."

"Okay."

"Do you know what your labor was last week?"

"Yes. Around twenty thousand without looking it up."

"That's kind of high, don't you think?"

"Not at all. I have forecasted out the month. My payroll will run around eighty thousand this month."

"Jeff. Kevin isn't going to like that and I also think that's too high."

"Jim, why don't you ask we how much I'll be billing at the end of the month."

"Okay. How much?"

"One million dollars. Which means our labor cost percentage will be eight percent of the totaled billed. That is also four percent under what has been estimated for the projects."

There was silence for a few moments.

"How do you know that?"

"Jim, I am the project manager. That is part of my responsibility to make sure the project is not only on time, but also at or below the estimated budget."

Another pause.

"I didn't know you were doing that."

"You do now. Is there still a problem with my payroll?

"Not at all. I'll let Kevin know when he calls me."

Usually a book keeper might be responsible for that information. Since I didn't have one and didn't want to wait on the home office to provide the information I needed on a day-to-day basis, I did it myself. Did I have to work longer hours? Yes, but I didn't mind because as I stated out in the earlier examples, when I was asked what was going on, I was prepared to deliver the correct information. My boss never questioned the payroll over the next two and-a-half years.

Folks, as long as you are prepared you will make your job and life a helluva lot easier and reduce your stress. Sounds like a win-win to me.

ACCOUNTABILITY

How many times have you gritted your teeth, refrained from biting your tongue off or restrained from pulling out every hair on your head or face because Joe, Bill, Jill or Sam refused to accept they screwed-up and either claimed ignorance or did their best to shuffle blame off to someone else? Come on, now. You know you've been around it. Hopefully you aren't one of those doing it. If so, you aren't going to like being called out, but you should be!

I was a project manager handling approximately eight different jobs out of the Dallas yard. They ranged in size from $150k to 15 million. The yard had over fifty pieces of equipment in it. I was working seven days a week, twelve to eighteen-hour days. Sometimes it would be a twenty-four-hour shift depending on the tasks being performed.

Sunday was my day to catch up on paperwork: payroll, invoices, driver logs and foremost, enter quantities from the prior week to know exactly how much work the crews had performed and what the end of the month estimate would look like. We are required to turn in an estimate on or before the 25th of each month so we can be paid on before the 20th of the following month.

I showed up and started going through quantities. It was quiet and peaceful. I stepped out to have a smoke and took an interest in one of the trucks parked in front of the trailer. All the equipment had a sticker for when the next oil change was due or in the case of larger equipment, how many hours till the next service.

Out of curiosity I went and checked out the truck's sticker. What I saw did not make me a happy camper. The unit was 5000 miles over due. 5000 miles! That, my friends, is unacceptable. Do that with your personnel vehicle and see how long it takes to blow the motor.

I looked around the yard and got this dreadful feeling in my gut as I looked at the equipment. Surely not. Surely the foreman have been keeping up with the service logs. As much as I wanted to believe they were, something told me they weren't. Only one way to find out. Check each and every piece in the yard and those out in the field.

Is this something I wanted to do? NO. Was it in my actual job description? NO! That aside, as a project manager everything that happens on my project is my responsibility.

Instead of getting my paperwork done, I spent the next ten hours going through every piece of equipment and checking the service logs, driver logs and cleanliness. How do you think I felt at 6:00pm Sunday evening? Let's just say, I could have bent nails with my teeth.

That aside, I had to develop a plan for the shop in Fort Worth on which machines and trucks needed to go immediately and be serviced. They could handle about four at a time. It would take two weeks to get everything caught up. So, I made up a list and faxed it over to the shop. This is going to make their Monday morning! And not only theirs.

Can anyone tell me where this is going? If you've read this far, you should have a good idea what type of managerial tool I'm going to use don't you? No? Well, think about it. Let's say our neighbor Sam or Jill borrowed your two-thousand-dollar riding lawn mower and returned it with a busted shaft and bent blade and then told you, "I don't know how it happened? I was mowing and it just broke." Are you kidding me? Just broke? Yeah, try again.

Oh, and they didn't offer to pay for the damages. Now, how are you going to react?

I'm going to use the only option available. And no, it isn't going to be a feel-good session with the foreman and their lead men. It's going to be an old-fashioned ass chewing in using very succinct and choice words.

Monday morning, the foreman and crews started arriving at 6:45am. I was there to greet them. When they asked what was on tab for the day I responded. "No one leaves the yard until I say so. Go to the safety trailer and wait."

You want to talk about stirring up a hornet's nest. The men couldn't believe I wasn't giving them their orders for the day and telling them to get out of my yard. I'm sure as more showed up and got the message, the gossip was running rife. I could care less. While they were congregating and trying to figure out what was going on, I was on the phone to the equipment manager lining up the critical pieces he needed to service first. He could not believe I had gone through all the equipment and then formed a battle plan to get everything fixed. I also informed him; it wouldn't happen again on my watch. If it did, that foreman would no longer be coming to the Dallas yard to work. He agreed wholeheartedly and wished the other project managers and superintendents would take the same steps.

Before I went into the meeting, it's important to point out that one of the biggest complaints the foreman had was that the shop in Fort Worth never fixed anything and when they did, they didn't do it right. Each foreman was provided with a repair request sheet in the weekly package that they were to fill out and give to the shop detailing problems with a particular piece of equipment. This too was about to change. I was to kill three birds with one stone!

I had them packed in the safety trailer like sardines. The trailer was built to hold twenty. I had over thirty in it. Yes, it was standing room only. I kept looking at my watch waiting for the last foreman to show up. He arrived at 7:45am a good hour late.

"Glad you could join us Bocho and hold up the meeting. Find a place to stand."

The tone of my voice gave them a good indication this wasn't going to be a friendly gathering.

I looked into the collection of men in front of me and stared each one down and no one in particular.

"Does anyone here know what I did yesterday?" Before they could answer I continued. "Instead of doing my job, I did yours! And to say the least I'm not a happy camper about it. I get one day to catch up on my paperwork to make sure you men get paid and that we get paid for the work we perform each month. But no. Instead of taking care of my business I wound up going through every piece of equipment in the yard and in the field to see how many were over do on service. Know what I found? Ninety percent of the equipment is overdue and that gentlemen, is your fault. Not mine. Not the superintendents. Not the shops-YOURS and only yours. This is unacceptable at any level. I would also like to add that the driver's logs have not been properly filled out. All of this stops today. I have already been on the phone to Jerry and Mark and given them a list of everything that needs to be updated. The most irritating thing about all of this is that you men have spent the last six months bitching and whining about the equipment not working. Did you fill out the work order and turn them in?"

I think someone tried to answer the question and I cut him off. This was a time for listening and not talking.

"In the future, all requests will be brought to my office and I will fax them to the shop. That way there will no excuses from the shop saying they didn't receive it or saying you dropped it off. I will have a record of the requests and will take care of the follow-up. Back to the equipment. I will not tolerate this lax attitude any more. You all claim to be grown men; start acting like it. Because as of right now, you're just a bunch of whiny school boys who need your asses whipped.

If this behavior doesn't change, I can guarantee you one thing, you will never work in the Dallas area again or on any of my projects. I will not tolerate laziness and apathy towards the equipment anymore. And, if you can't be to Dallas on time, don't bother showing up because I will send you right back to Fort Worth for reassignment! Any questions?"

One of the lead men had a question which was answered. None of the foreman said a word.

"Good. Go to work."

That was the quietest I ever heard these men while they gathered up their tools and supplies. To top it off, the radio and phone was very silent that day and I caught up on all the work I didn't complete on Sunday!

My actions might seem harsh and over the top but the desired result was achieved: foreman made sure vehicles were serviced on time, driver's logs were properly filled out, repair requests came in when a problem was identified, the shop repaired what we sent and everyone was on time! Remember when I said I was killing three birds with one stone? We wound up getting five. That my friends, is an effective management meeting.

I know this strategy isn't for everyone and in the politically correct/HR era its highly doubtful it would be accepted, but in my field, it worked and results is what we are after.

My advice is, I can use harsh language in my field. I'm sure each industry has its own nomenclature that is more apropos. Use it to your advantage when your employees become brain dead. They will listen or leave.

Jeff Dawson

BAD ADVICE, INCOMPETETNS AND BROWN NOSERS

It doesn't matter what industry you're in. These people are like the plague. They show up with false intentions and then infect everyone around them. On the surface they are the nicest people you'll ever meet. Their sincerity is skin deep and their knowledge is right along with their sincerity-shallow.

They will come across in the interview as the brightest person you've ever met. You'll keep thinking to yourself, "Why hasn't anyone hired them before? They will be a perfect fit." Believe me, there's a reason they aren't working.

I've had the dishonor of working with three of these fine individuals.

I partnered with two other men and formed a company. One caveat, I would be office sharing with the home company's accountant-self-proclaimed general contractor.

We are concentrating on public work projects with a sampling of private work. See, with a public job you know you are going to get paid, some time. A private job, not so much. Sure, you can file liens and get judgements, but in the end, good luck collecting. Alright, back on track.

I found a job in Highland Park that was perfect for our start-up. Project size was coming in at 1.2 million. A good solid price. The advisor came into my office and asked what I was sitting at. I told him right at 1.2 million.

"That's too high. Bonding company will only cover one million."

"Then tell them to raise the limit for the job and we'll be okay."

"No. Cut the price to one million and we'll worry about it later when we price the job out.""

One. Who in the hell is we? And on the civil side, we don't go to Wal-Mart or Target for the best deal. Prices are submitted and that's what we go in with. That is not the case with GC's and private jobs. They will shop till the subcontractors drop. This would be strike one.

We were low on the project. Left $150,000 on the table! That is an unacceptable amount of money for that time. The only one concerned was me.

Now, to top it off, I had to hire a solid pipe foreman. Not a problem. Put out the ad and received several calls and emails. The first one hired lasted a week. He was too good to get out of his truck. Seriously? If you want to be a pick-up truck seat superintendent, look elsewhere.

The second candidate was more than qualified. I knew him from another company we worked for. Only problem and this is a dumb one, he wanted more money than I was making. This is the one time I let my ego interfere with a solid business decision. He would have been worth every penny in the long run.

I wound up hiring Mike. Solid resume. Knew his passed employer. Solid company and brought him onboard.

The first sign something was off was when I talked to his past employer. There isn't a lot of information companies can share today about employees because of the HR bullshit. I asked why he left. They didn't know. Odd. Okay. Thank you.

Why would someone leave a solid, established, well known, financially sound and excellent benefits company for a start up? I would find out.

Project started out well enough. Mike took his set of plans and laid a battle plan. I approved and we moved forward. After a month he still hadn't put in one joint of pipe. I understood the city was being anal about locating every line that we might come in contact with. Okay, no problem. Plus, he was putting a new crew together. Cutting your teeth can take a bit of time.

By month three. I believe he had four joints of storm drain in. Again, I understand the challenges of crossing a street and traffic switches. Still, production is way behind and I'm beginning to get concerned.

When I wasn't checking on the project, I was bidding other jobs and starting to get on a hot streak. Thus, I could not devote all of my time to one project. That's what I had a foreman for, or so goes the thinking.

The project rocked along losing money every day. That's right. Losing money every day! The company advisor called the other two owners to Dallas for an update. He told them everything was going fine. I told him I disagreed. My comment was brushed off. Okay.

By the sixth month, I'd had enough. The storm drain was finished yet the sewer line work hadn't started. Mike showed me his plan of attack for at least the fourth time. My reply, "I don't give two shits about your drawings. It's time to get some pipe in the ground or find a different job. That worked for about a month. Progress was being made but at a painful pace.

We had enough jobs going now that they were starting to stack up on each other because Mike couldn't get it together. I had reached the end of my rope. I need a solid pipe foreman. I found him and instead of firing Mike, I made another huge mistake, I promoted him to general superintendent. Don't ask me what I was thinking. I wasn't!

This was an epic disaster. I had three other crews working and they knew how poor Mike's production was. The best reason I can give, looking back is, I was overtaxed and not thinking straight.

It just wasn't the Highland Park job going in the tank, it was every job he touched. The red ink was so deep, you could have drowned a giraffe in it!

Jeff Dawson

When the advisor finally realized the situation the company was in, he conveniently washed his hands of the venture and blamed me for all of the problems. Okay, I'm man enough to admit I made a host of mistakes. That falls on me. I made a horrible decision in hiring Mike and didn't cut him loose fast enough. Couple my poor judgement and having the advisor cut my price $200k was a recipe for disaster. The project lost $150,000 when it was completed.

So what lessons are to be learned?

1) I should have fired Mike after the second month.
2) I should have been more involved in the day-to-day field operations until I was comfortable the project was on track.
3) I should have bid less work and managed better
4) I should have continued to look for a competent foreman

5) And, I should have held my ground with the initial price I worked-up or not bid the job.

The point here is being accountable for my bad decisions and not making those mistakes ever again. Who's with me?

Now let's talk about the brown nosers. Every company has one to two or maybe more than you can count. These employees are the worst and when you identity them, there are no second chances. They must go.

I hired a man to be a general laborer. At this point and time, remember when I talked about the equipment faux-pas, I needed someone to make sure all the equipment was being greased daily. The foreman were doing better but I didn't want us to slide backwards. He didn't care about working long hours.

When he wasn't checking on the equipment, he was cleaning the yard, keeping up with the material inventory or shuttling equipment from Dallas to Fort Worth. This took a huge burden off my superintendent and me.

The first two months went by smoothly, but I could tell he was looking for something else. He was spending more time around my office than he should. Why? Simple. He was trying to get in good with the boss and then play a card about more money and a better position.

The dirt foreman came into my office, uninvited and started ragging me about Bill. I listened to him for all of ten seconds and told him to worry about himself because if he had time to watch what Bill was doing, then he wasn't doing his job. I also told him that with Bill on payroll he was maintaining and servicing the equipment for his crew. That shut him up and he left.

Another month passed and Bill was doing exactly what I thought would happen. He was coming in late about once a week and had to leave early, once a week. The yard was staying clean. Inventory was lacking and he would disappear for a couple of hours in the company truck.

His behavior was becoming a problem not only with me but my superintendent and some of the other workers.

I asked Bill to take care of a task that would take about two hours to perform. At the end of two hours, it still wasn't done. I called him to my office and fired him on the spot. I went out to the jobsite to meet with the state.

When I returned in an hour or so, he was still on property waiting for his ride. Remember Jose? He was in the yard with a strange look on his face.

"Jeff. Bill called me and wanted to know if he could work for me." He said in a cautionary tone.

"Hell, no he can't. He's fired and that's that!"

Jose looked at Bill and said nothing.

I looked at Bill and told him, "I fired you. You can wait for your ride outside the gate."

I went back into my office and went back to work. Never heard another word from him, which was a good thing.

I saw the cancer growing and knew it was time to cut it out. Some might think I was a bit too harsh. Too bad. The problem would have only gotten worse and the morale of the crews would have deteriorated. I had worked too hard to let one person unravel the works.

Bottom line, when you identify them, get rid of them immediately or your job will become a nightmare.

CONFRONTATION AND RESPECT

For whatever reason these words seem to strike fear in managers. Everyone wants to be the nice guy or gal and be friends with employees or even worse, they might hurt some one's feelings. Well, get over it. If you want to be a solid manager that your employees respect, you better get tough and real fast. Here is why.

I took a job with a company in Fort Worth-Project Manager on the 635 ITS (Intelligent Traffic System). I 'd been with the company for a couple of months, still getting my feet wet and waiting for the contractor to give us the go ahead to start making dirt fly. I spent this time wisely getting to know the company, how it operated and the men I would be working with. John, my superintendent was a good-natured knowledgeable man who knew his way around a highway job. He'd been an inspector with TXDOT for five years. He'd also worked for various companies performing the same type of work we'd been contracted to perform. His only weakness was he wanted to do the work instead of helping supervise it. This I would work on.

There was another superintendent who was the "chosen one" of the owner. Everyone who mentioned his name said I was in for a real education. Jose can do whatever he wants and there's nothing you can do about it. I made a mental note and waited to meet him. Didn't have long to wait.

Two weeks later, Jose came to my office trailer and attempted to tell me how the job was going to be run. The conversation went something like this.

"I'm, Jose and I run the field. I don't care what you do in the office but you don't come out in the field to see or tell me or my people what to do. I'll handle it."

I digested his words for a few moments,

"Jose, I don't give a damn who you are or what you want. I was hired to run this job and that's what I'm going to do. If you have a problem with that, too bad. Now, get out of my office and we'll discuss this with the owner of the company."

As he walked out, I heard him say, "The owner will back me up." We'll see.

I called the owner and told him he, Jose, John and I need to have a meeting immediately. It was set-up for the next day at 2:30pm.

I informed John and Jose of the meeting. Jose hung up on me.

We three arrived at the office on time and were escorted into the owner's office. Kevin, the owner did not know what was about to transpire. That worked in my favor.

We all sat down.

"Jeff, is there a problem?" asked Kevin.

"Yes. I need to know who's in charge of the job. Jose or me. I signed a contract with your company to be the project manager for this job. Jose says he is the project manager and John and I have no business going out on the jobsite to see what's going on. I need to know right now who's running the job. Jose or me."

He was not ready for this confrontation, but here it was. I was either going to get fired or perform the duties I was hired for. Some might have called the lull uncomfortable silence. I viewed it as a man faced with a dilemma that had to be resolved immediately.

He looked at the three of us. "Jeff. You're in charge." His voice was almost too low to be audible.

"Mr. Kevin. Would you make sure that Jose understands what you just said."

"Jose, Jeff is in charge and John is his superintendent. Together, they are responsible for the project. "

And that was it. The groundwork had been set and the confrontation put to rest.

Now, don't' think that made for smooth sailing all the time. Jose resented that I had challenged his authority and the owner had backed me up instead of him. What it did accomplish, as I would find out later, a ton of respect from the men and crews I would work with over the coming years. They found out I wouldn't sit on my hands and just let things slide. If there was a problem with employees or technical matters, they were both addressed with the utmost speed and diligence.

The one person I didn't think would come around was Jose. As I mentioned earlier, we would be working together on this and other projects.

Jose called me one afternoon. He had a problem and couldn't figure it out. He was doing a directional bore under a box culvert. He knew the bore was going straight yet the sensor showed the drill head was seven feet off line.

I looked the situation over and suggested he keep drilling. 'Let's go another ten feet and see where you pick the signal up."

He wasn't sure about the decision, yet he knew with me onsite, if something went wrong, it wouldn't be his fault.

The operator drilled another ten feet and guess where we located the drill head? You got it. Seven feet off line. This made the fourth mark seven feet off the line. So, the question is, whey were we getting a false signal? Box culverts are full of steel. I had talked to the bore crews over the past year learning the trade. One of thing I picked up was how steel deflected the signal.

"Jose. The steel is reflecting the signal. Keep drilling like you're doing and the drill head will pop out on the other side maybe one foot off line."

"Are you sure?"

"Yes."

That was a major break-through for both of us. He began to trust and respect my knowledge while I learned to let the past go and move forward. I'm happy to say that all the projects, he, John and I were in charge of all made money and a lot of it.

If we wouldn't have had that uncomfortable meeting in the beginning, I seriously doubt we would have been a successful organization.

I need to backtrack just a bit with the Jose situation. Most of what I am detailing deals with a group of people. What do you do when faced with a situation where embarrassing the employee would not be in anyone's interest? Simple, you handle it one-on-one.

John and I had set up a tutorial for the men on setting up drill shaft anchor bolts. Most of you haven't seen this. Those structures you see on the highway with a message board or the exit sign have a drill shaft with pier steel and a set of anchor bolts we attach the structure to.

There is a special way to set the form and brace the anchor bolts. At the time, we were short on manpower and decided to have a tutorial out on IH 635 and train about twelve men on how the process works. We knew one day wouldn't make them experts. Only time and repetitive actions would make them proficient in it, but at least they would have a good idea how to assist in the process if we needed them to lend a hand.

I was at the office handling paperwork. John was onsite working with the men. Every thing was going smooth and then my phone rang.

"I quit! I'm sick of this crap."

"What's the problem?"

"Jose. That damn, Jose. I can't work with him anymore!"

"John. Calm down and come to the office. I need to know what happened."

He showed up and told me Jose was taking pictures of all the men standing around learning how to do the job. He was convinced Jose was trying to set John and me up. He would show the pictures to Kevin and hope we would be fired. Granted, this was an assumption on our part, but it seemed logical.

I called Jose on the radio and told him to get to my office immediately.

This is how that discussion went when he showed up.

"Jose. I'll only say this once. John is going quit because of you and I need him a helluva a lot more than I need you. Have you forgotten who Kevin said was in charge of this job?"

"No."

"Good. Now, I don't care what it takes but you will fix this with John right now. John, I want you to tell Jose exactly what is on your mind."

Over the next five minutes I let them hash out their problems and come to an agreement. When I felt they were finished, I stepped in.

"Okay, from this day forward, am I going have any more issues with you two? Are we going to work together or keep butting heads?"

They both responded in the affirmative.

"Good. One last thing I want to say is this, it stops right here. I don't want either one of you talking to anyone else about what happened today. Understood?"

They agreed.

"Good. Now, get the hell off my yard so I can get my work done."

The point here is simple, if you have an issue with an employee or two employees that have taken issue with each other, don't' dodge it. Get the parties together and resolve the issues before it festers to a boiling point and then all hell breaks loose. If you don't have the backbone to handle this type of situation, then you shouldn't be a manager-period.

I'm happy to say, from this point on, there were no more "Come to Jesus Meetings" on this issue. We worked together and tackled any problem that came our way and resolved it.

Another scenario is when I attended a Sci-Fi convention in Dallas and was asked to be on a discussion panel. Of course, I said yes.

I forgot what the topic was, but that doesn't matter. What does matter is what happens when you have a lousy moderator in charge.

How many have been to a meeting that you knew was going to be a waste of time and energy after they spoke the first few words?

There were five or six of us on the panel. We each took about thirty seconds to a minute introducing ourselves and a quick rundown of books we had written. So far, so good.

Then the moderator/facilitator/egocentric/keynote speaker began talking and talking and talking and talking. Remember, this is a fifty-minute panel. No more. That's it!

I looked down at my watch a few times wondering when he was going to shut-up. He didn't. He kept self-promoting himself to the point, I think the cows actually came home!

During his boring monologue, at least three or four people kept raising their hands to ask a question on a particular point. He ignored them and kept talking.

Has anyone ever been in this situation before? How did you react?

This is how I reacted

With only thirty minutes left and a room full of people, I'd had enough. I guess the guy took a breath or was trying to formulate some other tangent no one gave two shits about. I grabbed the opportunity.

"Are we here to listen to you talk or to answer questions? I believe it's the latter. It's time to start taking questions."

The look on his face was priceless! He got so flustered he didn't know what to do. He did attempt to regain his composure.

"I'm the moderator of this panel and will conduct it as I see fit."

"Fine. Then stop talking and start taking questions. That's what we're all here for."

And yes, we took questions for the next twenty-five minutes.

The point is simple, if you are hosting an event make sure your speaker stays on point and doesn't ramble. Nothing kills a presentation/seminar more than a speaker who only thinks about themselves and their compensation.

Now, if you're the speaker, it's all the more important to stay on point!

One more scenario is well worth mentioning. This one is a little unusual in that it deals with chewing out the client, constructively and coming out on top.

We were performing a project at DFW airport. It was a labor only contract. Prime contractor made the grade, tied the steel, supplied the forms, belt placers, trucks and concrete. Our portion was setting the forms, placing and finishing the concrete. It was a sweet job to say the least.

We had been working about two weeks on the project. Everything was working like a well- oiled machine. While we did the hand pours the prime was taking care of the slip-form work. We were having zero problems. That was about to change and not in a good way.

My superintendent called up. "Jeff, we have a problem."

"Okay. What is the problem?'

"Randy is pissed."

"What did you do to piss him off?"

"Nothing."

"Okay. Then why is he pissed?"

"You need to come out here and handle it. He's mad at us."

"Why?"

"Just get out here and take care of it."

He hung up. Okay, what could we have done to piss him off? I rolled over and over in my mind what we could have possibly done. I was clueless.

When I pulled up on the job. I saw Randy and could immediately tell he was upset.

"How's it going Randy."

"Not worth a damn."

"What's the problem?"

"You and your company."

"Randy, what in the hell have we done? Did Jose or I say or do something wrong?"

"No."

Okay, now I'm getting frustrated. "Randy. If Jose and I haven't done anything wrong, then what in the hell is the matter?"

He looked down at the ground, kicked up some dirt and lit up a cigarette. "My bosses were out here today."

"And?

"They told me my crew didn't know how to pour concrete and that your crew is making me look bad."

"They said what?!"

"That your crew is better than mine and if they had a right mind, they'd hire all of your men to finish the job."

"Who said this? Was it Jim?"

"Yes."

"How long ago was this?"

"About an hour or so ago."

"Randy. I promise you this, I will fix the problem before the day is over. We have too good of a working relationship for it to go to hell. I promise, I'll fix this."

"You better."

Jim is the VP/Project Manger of the Company. I have known him since college days and we had done a few jobs in the past. That aside, what he just did was unacceptable. I didn't care how big the company was. He just created an intolerable work atmosphere that could derail the entire project.

I need to point one other item out. A slip form paver is a large paving machine that performs all the heavy lifting when it comes to pouring concrete. You've probably seen them once or twice driving on the highway on highway project or even some city streets, wondering what that big machine was doing. The men working around the paver are there to make sure it is working properly and that the concrete coming out the back is on the correct grade and finish. Hand work, what we do, is exactly that. We set the forms, tie the steel, shovel the concrete in front of the screed, vibrate with hand vibrators, use 16' straight edges and channel floats to smooth it, build the curb with shovels and mules, drag a tine rake for the finish then spray curing compound on the finished product. Can you see where this is going?

I called Jim.

"Jim. This is Jeff."

"What can I do for, Jeff."

"Did you and some of your bosses come out to the jobsite this morning."

"Yes."

"Did you or someone with you tell Randy my crew was better than yours?"

There was pause. "Jim. Did someone say that?"

"Yes."

"Why in the hell would someone say that? Do you have any idea what is going on out here right now?"

"No."

"Let me tell you, it isn't good. Randy is no longer going to work with us. He's so mad he could eat nails or even worse, quit! Jim, you cannot compare Randy's crew to mine any more than I can compare mine to his. It is like comparing apples to oranges. My crew does this type of work day in and day out. It is physically demanding. His crew works behind a belt placer, paving machine, work bridge, tine machine and a cure rig. They are not physically capable of doing what we do on a day-to-day basis. And, if I put my crew behind your paver, I guarantee they will screw it up. I've tried in the past with miserable results. They don't grasp the concept that machines are capable of doing the work. Since I've done both, I know the difference, but I'll never get these guys to understand that."

He's still listening.

"Now, is the project on schedule?"

"Yes."

"Is your company making money?"

"Yes."

"Do you want us to continue working harmoniously?"

"Yes."

"Then call Randy and fix this."

About an hour later I went back to the jobsite. Randy was standing by his truck with a small smile.

"How's it going, Randy."

"Good. Did you really call Jim and lay into him?"

"I did. I told him what they did to you this morning was ridiculous and uncalled for. You have one type of crew and I another. Even though they are both concrete crews, we work differently. Now, do we still have a good working relationship?"

"Yes, we do."

There are two lessons to take away from this: If you're the manager before you start looking for excuses on employee performance, make damn sure it's what they are good at and if you're a subcontractor and you have created a solid working relationship with the company's supervisor, do not hesitate to call out upper management when they interfere and almost derail the project.

Jeff Dawson

TEAM-MY ASS!

Of all of the buzz words today this is the one that I cannot stand! Why, you might ask. Simple. The word is overused and is another con job some business school came up with and then did a snow job on companies convincing them this is the way it out to be. Really?

It's right up there with the "power ties" of the eighties, air quotes and let us not forget, "thinking outside the box." What a bunch of crap!

When the word "Team" is used, I expect to see everyone in a uniform competing for a championship, not showing up and doing your job. It seems like there is a similar correlation between the two but upon further analysis they couldn't be any more opposite than night or day. I have yet to be on a jobsite where there are cheerleaders yelling, "GO TEAM, GO" or an employee forming a gaggle and trying to ramp everyone up. And the day I do, is the day I'm getting out of the business! We are professionals that were hired to perform our duties to the best of our capabilities. It is necessary to lay out ground work and develop an overall plan to tackle a project and then keep everyone involved in the process. Unlike a sports organization, we don't have Spring Training or warm-up games. We hit the street running and better be ready to handle it or else.

When you are part of a sports team, you have an assigned duty. Correct? If you're a pitcher or a quarterback you know what your duties are. Throw the ball over the plate and get batters out or hand off or throw the ball to a receiver in the hopes of putting your team in the best position to win the game. Correct?

Businesses resemble a band more than anything. Ever heard of a band being called a team? What about an orchestra or a symphony? Never thought of it that way, have you? You can also throw marching bands and cheerleaders into this group.

They are made up of squads or sections. Depending on the group, each member is responsible for a particular part of the music or activity. They must practice their assignment until they have mastered it. Yet at the same time, they have to add their talents to the collective group and put the pieces together into a harmonious performance or routine. When someone makes a mistake the section or squad leader is responsible for calling it out and working with that individual until they master the routine. And if they can't do it, then they find someone on the squad who can assist.

When I was in the jazz band, even though I was first chair, I did not have a musical ear and could not improvise to save my life. The band got together and agreed we should meet at Margaret's house for an impromptu practice. What I didn't know is they were putting it together for me. At least five of the musicians in the group tutored me on how to hear the chords and blend in with the rest of the band. I will not say I became proficient at it, but with their, guidance and support, I didn't embarrass myself or the band when it time for me to solo. That is great leadership and mentoring.

In business, especially construction, if you think you only have one job to perform, you have been sadly misinformed! As a project manager your duties are not limited to only: payroll, material inventory, scheduling, ordering material, equipment maintenance, TXDOT driver logs, new hires and of course, problem solving. You also have to have a keen desire to continue learning new techniques and procedures, for the industry is always evolving. In sports, rules change but overall the game has not. What's harder to do, build a bridge over live traffic, a river or identifying a blitz or curveball? Is it easier to run eighty yards for a touchdown or pour concrete on an active tarmac? Is it easier to nail a goal from twenty yards out or organize a 300K arms deal? Tell me again how businesses are a team? They are not.

If your company uses the term and it has no effect, then drop it immediately! Enough said.

CHURCH SOCIAL

What in the world could this be about? Well, I'm sure it's not what you're thinking. To me, this can be one of the most damaging acts that can occur at a company. Some might call it water cooler talk or the smoke break brigade. All of those would be correct for they all describe the same thing-company "bullshit" gossip.

When I accepted the job in Dallas, I had no idea how big the company was or how many different offices there were.

After a few months I learned we had offices in San Antonio, Houston, Corpus Cristi, Austin, Fort Worth and of course, the new Dallas office. For me, that was no big deal. It let me know that the company was diversified and stable. That's a good thing.

My superintendent, John, had worked for the company about ten years ago so he kind of knew the climate of the company but didn't dwell on it too much. I would soon get the crash course.

It was around five months before we could aggressively get the job under way. At first. We would get one crew which consisted of three men. Not a big deal to manage. As time progressed, we had four to ten full time crews at any one time. This is where it started getting interesting as I met all the different foreman and their characteristics. While that in itself can be challenging it was the garbage, they would bring onto the jobsite that began troubling me. All of them had worked at the different offices and had nothing flattering to say. One foreman in-particular complained about all of them. Seriously, he had nothing good to say about any of them, including the Dallas office. What the hell? I haven't done anything to provoke this type of attitude.

I let it go on for a few months until enough was enough. The projects were moving along smoothly and I wasn't about to let them get derailed.

All the crews showed up one morning and were preparing to go to work. I overhead them talking about Austin, Houston, etc. This was utter bullshit and I wasn't hearing it anymore.

I pulled all the foreman into my office trailer. Packed 'em in like sardines!

I wasted no time and minced no works.

"Gentlemen, as of today I don't want to hear one more word about Austin, San Antonio, Houston, Corpus Christ or Fort Worth. I am sick and tired of hearing about the bitching, whining and complaining. It stops today. You leave that shit at the gate. Do you understand?"

Let's say there was some grumblings amongst them.

"Here's why I don't want to hear that shit anymore. The last thing I want is for the other offices to start gossiping about us. Every time I hear this incessant complaining it reminds of a bunch of "church social backstabbing bitches." You are accomplishing nothing and pissing me off. When you come through that gate you are on my time and my schedule. Got it? The only thing I want to hear on the Grapevine is that we are doing our job, doing it well and making money. That's it nothing else. You are all grown men now start acting like it! Questions?"

There were none.

"Good. Get to work."

From that point on the only idle chatter I overheard was job related and how to tackle problems. That is what I was after and it worked!

I know my words and actions can be a bit harsh at times, so depending on your industry, you might have to soften the words somewhat. Still, if you don't address it, it will only get worse and instead of completing the tasks at hand, a lot of time is going to be wasted for no good reason because Jimmy or Suzy got their feelings hurt because Joe and Jill said Bill didn't think they were capable of doing their jobs and sooner or later Bruce would hear about it.

If you can follow that logic, then you are one of the problems and need to cease it immediately!

Jeff Dawson

BAD BOSSES

This subject matter is and can be a bit touchy. There are plenty of successful firms out there that have some of the worst owners or managers than you can count. They treat their employees like crap. Don't let them advance. Never acknowledge your efforts and are the first to accept accolades and praise while ignoring that it was the employees who made the success possible. They are also the first to deny raises and bonuses and last but not least, the first to tell let their employees know how useless they are and questions why you were hired in the first place.

If you can relate or work at a company like this, get out now. Your talents will be recognized by a company that will appreciate your hard work and dedication. If there isn't one in your industry, then try starting your own.

The best example I have for this is my father, RIP 2-15-2005. Dad worked his ass off for DuPont and loved it. He started in a chemical plant and wound up selling explosives to contractors and rock quarries. He was the top man in his field and that isn't bragging, that's the truth.

His boss is another story. DuPont was thinking of downsizing and the explosive division was going to be phased out. His boss, informed dad that if he took early retirement, he would get a hefty raise, which was long overdue, and that would enhance his retirement package.

I did meet my dad's boss several times and didn't have a high opinion of him at all. He came across as a snake-in-the-grass and he didn't disappoint me. See, if it weren't for dad, Bob had no real function with the company other than drawing an exorbitant income and taking credit for all of Dad's hard work.

Dad retired and found that Bob never turned in the promised raise. He wound up giving himself the raise! Shocking. Was Dad upset? A little, but after thirty-five years he wouldn't say anything derogatory about his employer. It had been a good run and after all, the company had taken care of Dad and his family.

This type of manager is the worst! Know anyone like that?

Another good example is the employer I had in Dallas. I signed an employee contract with well spelled out bonus clauses. After being with them for nine months, the VP of Operations wanted to meet with me. Instead of one job, as per the contract, he wanted me take on another project. I agreed for an additional 20K a year. I should have had the agreement revised, but I took it on a handshake.

In February of 2010, two weeks before I was to undergo extensive back surgery, the company released me. The reason I was given was pure BS. The company was scaling back and my services were no longer needed. Really? The company has more work than they can handle and needed every available hand on deck. I was released because they had brought up a Vice-President from Houston because they were slow. He didn't like me and I sure as hell didn't like him!

So, what happened to all the bonus money in my contract? I had to sue the company. Why? Why was it necessary to take such drastic action? Simple, the higher ups in management and the owner wanted to keep all of that money, to the tune of 350K!

Jeff Dawson

LET'S HAVE A BEER

Being in construction does have an advantage if you like to drink, beer is plentiful. I thought I drank a lot in college. What a misnomer on my part. I had no idea how much Mexicans could drink! I was a novice.

While on the surface it seems like a good idea to mingle with the help; it is a double- edged sword.

I had the foresight to realize that even though I was socializing with the workers, I was still their boss and that wasn't going to change anytime soon. And it didn't. If I was going to attend one of the parties, work was not allowed to be discussed at all. We were there to eat, drink and have fun and that's it. You see, there's a time and place for everything. You have to know how to separate them.

I've seen too many instances where employees are rubbing elbows with the big boys or girls and think that once the alcohol starts flowing, they can and will say whatever comes to mind. This is a major mistake! What you say can and will be used against you. They get too comfortable and issues that should be discussed at the office or one-on-one start percolating out revealing exactly what the employee thinks about management, because they assume, they are buds when they are not. Let me say that again, they are not your friend, he or she is your boss.

Let's shift to another scenario for a moment where alcohol was involved. I was going to a job interview at one of the nicer topless joints in Dallas. Even though I was a frequent member of some of the other clubs, I wasn't comfortable having a job interview at this venue. As I've stated before, there is a time and a place for everything and this isn't the time or the place for business.

Within in an hour the guy who was interviewing me was drunk. This is strike two. When he insisted I have a table dance, that was strike three. I should have walked out at that time. Instead of strike three, it must have been a foul tip because I was still swinging away.

Somewhere in the two or three hours we talked, we went over my qualifications and strong suits. My weakness is the commercial side. I've built roads, bridges, underground lines and the like. I have never been in charge of a slab on grade building. I remember telling him, don't put me on one of those projects unless I have a strong superintendent who can show me the ropes so I don't screw things up. Can you guess where this is headed? You are correct. They put me on a three-school project in Waxahachie without a superintendent. The one who was down there asked me what I was there for. "To manage these three schools." "I don't need a manager; I need a working foreman." To top that off, I pissed off the general contractor the first week. How long do you think I stayed with that job? I think it was a couple of months. I was put in a position to fail from the start. I never, ever, ever accepted or attended a job interview where alcohol or topless dancers are found. It was a recipe for disaster and that's exactly what happened. So, if you think it's a good idea to condone this behavior, trust me, you are being set up for failure. Is that what you want?

So, how can you mix the two, if at all? It's simple. As I stated earlier, work is off limits when it comes to spending down time with the employees.

I have been friends with my superintendent for over thirty years and his family. We've had good times and a few bad times, but we are able to separate work from socializing. We might mention a job or two and then catch ourselves and start talking sports or how our kids are doing. That's what were there for. We can discuss work any other time.

Just remember, there is nothing wrong with having a cold one with the guys/girls now and then, but if you want to make it a habit, you might start looking for a different employer.

LIVE TO WORK, WORK TO LIVE?
(That is the question)

This is one of the most, if not, THE most important chapter of this book.

In 2004 I went broke for the second time in my life. I moved back in with my parents to regroup. When I arrived in Tulsa, I found out my father had terminal cancer. He was expected to live seven months. Instead of pursuing a job, I had the honor of taking care of my father through this difficult time. After he passed in February of 2005 I actively began searching for a job. It took over a year to finally land one in Dallas. Yep, I was going back to Texas.

I convinced myself that this was going to be a great opportunity to learn and grow at age forty-six, and it was.

For the first three years, I busted my ass! I lived, ate and sometimes slept at the office. I knew it would be a demanding assignment and I would be working at least six days a week twelve-hour-days. I was wrong. It became seven days a week and twenty-hour days. Since we were working days and nights, I might work three days straight before getting any rest. I know, that's not the smartest thing to do, but I was in the zone. How many of you can relate?

All of that would change in 2009 and drastically!

I dated a girl in high school, Debbie Beck, from 77 to 78. I went off to college and you can imagine the rest. It was a nasty break-up that took over a year to get over. Damn, I loved that girl.

Like many of us, I married, had kids and went to work. The marriage ended in divorce and I got the kids and the company. I dated other women through the years but I never could get Debbie out of my mind. That's right, even when I was married.

Bear with me; I have a point to all of this.

In 2009 I put a business card in her parent's mailbox. It was two weeks before I heard from her. That was a great day. Waited thirty years to talk to her again.

She lived in McAlister, Oklahoma which is two-and-a-half hours from Dallas. I didn't know if anything would come of it, but I had to make sure.

I went to visit her and yes, there was still a spark from all those years gone by.

As our relationship grew, something strange started taking place, work was no longer my priority. It was Debbie and her girls. See, she was on the tail end of radiation therapy from breast cancer. She tried everything she could to discourage me from coming up: bald, chemo, divorced, radiation treatment, etc. It didn't matter to me.

It took the guys and my bosses some time to realize that I had a different priority and it wasn't work. I went from working seven days a week to five and sometime four-and-a-half days a week. Now, you might ask, "how were you able to still be efficient and perform your duties?" Simple. I pulled my head out and started living life!

If we don't work, it's kind of difficult to pay the bills, but it's even more rewarding when you're able to enjoy the fruits of your labor with the ones you love and not those who provide a paycheck and will replace you at the drop of a hat.

I'd like to say this had a happy ending, but then that's only in fairy tales. Debbie passed in July of 2010 after her breast cancer returned.

She taught me two important life lessons I'll never forgot: Take care of unfinished business and work to live, not live to work.

Need I say more?

PRAISE

Now that I've ripped you up one side and down the other, its time reflect on the results. Call it praise, call it positive reinforcement or job well done. I don't care what you call it, but you damn well have to acknowledge it and let the employees know they aren't just a number on the payroll, they are an integral part of the process and deserve to be recognized!

Seriously, what is the point of busting your ass, meeting deadlines, being prepared if your boss is going to take all the credit? Honestly, I can't think of one reason. I understand needing a paycheck, but at what cost? Your sanity? Your self-worth and esteem? How many people do you know that absolutely hate their job and their employer because no matter what they do, they are never acknowledged for their hard work?

Is it that hard for you to pat your employees on the back and tell them what a great job they are doing? Is it that hard to give them an unexpected gift card to a nice restaurant showing your appreciation? Is it that hard to put in a raise for them or if you're the owner, provide a nice bonus and raise? If it is, I bet your turnover rate is high and overall company morale is low. None of these are formulas for a successful operation.

I never flinched when it came to calling out an employee for doing an outstanding job and requesting a raise for them.

Bottom line, if you want to keep good employees and they are excellent producers then show them!

AFTERMATH

So, what did you think? I know this probably isn't the most in depth work you've read; it wasn't supposed to be. For me, the more words one has to read the easier it is for the message to be lost or glossed over.

What I hope you got out of this is, eliminate political correctness, work for good people, be an engaging speaker and when confronted with an issue, do your homework, be prepared, stick to your guns and if you make a mistake own up to it and move on.

It really is that simple.

If you'd like to book a speaking engagement, email me at lddjenterprises@gmail.com or jdawson41@netzero.net.

Jeff Dawson

If you enjoyed the story, please do not hesitate to post a review on Amazon, Goodreads or any other site of preference.

Other works include:
Gateway: Pioche, Science fiction
Destination D.C. Book two of the Gateway series
Target Berlin Book three of the Gateway series
Occupation, WWII Alternative history
Sabotage Book two
Terror at the Sterling, horror
Love's True Second Chance, Memoir
Why Did Everything Happen?, Memoir
The Baseball Coaching Manual: Little League to High School. Volumes I & II, Instructional
Goober and Bill, Humor
Final Delivery, Suspense short
Women of War-poetry
Irving Titans-NFL satire

Other works available through LDDJ Enterprises Publishing
Angelic Answers: Love Letter for Daily Life, Kathryn Magee, Spiritual

You can follow me at:
Twitter: @Jeff Dawson59
Facebook: https://www.facebook.com/jeff.dawson.184 or https://www.facebook.com/pages/Loves-True-Second-Chance/201274679901838
Facebook: https://www.facebook.com/pages/Why-did-everything-happen/146270185426560?ref=hl
Website: http://jeff-dawson.blogspot.com/
Email: LDDJEnterprises@gmail.com

Jeff Dawson

Amazon link: http://www.amazon.com/Jeff-Dawson/e/B0054DRYIO/ref=sr_tc_2_0?qid=1394463163&sr=1-2-ent

Upcoming releases:
Cauldron: 3rd book in the Occupation series Fall release

www.ingramcontent.com/pod-product-compliance
Lightning Source LLC
Chambersburg PA
CBHW051347040426
42453CB00007B/451